The A

MW00986085

How To Master And Use Subterfuge On Anyone

By Madison Taylor

Table of Contents

Chapter 1: Why We Lie

It is a common Judeo-Christian ethic that lying and deception is not appropriate or nice behavior. Indeed, it can be very hurtful when you find that someone has lied to you. But deception exists for a reason. It serves many useful purposes in life. Therefore, the art of a deception is a useful art to learn.

This book is your guide to the art of deception. You will learn how to effectively deceive others without getting caught. You will also learn when it is acceptable to lie, so that you do not feel guilty for lying when you have to. This book will teach you skills and ways to avoid detection while you are employing deception.

Arguing about whether or not deception is morally wrong is beyond the scope of this book. However, most people can agree that deception is a natural part of human nature. We can strive to be moral all we want, but there are some situations where lying is just absolutely necessary.

You have probably already encountered many situations where deception is necessary. There are many times when lying is socially acceptable and necessary. Honesty is not always the best policy in these scenarios. You may not want to hurt someone's feelings. You may want to protect yourself or get out of a dangerous situation. You may want something, but you must lie to get it. Some studies have even found that lying to your spouse or romantic partner is necessary for the health of the overall relationship. Sometimes, you may even find that lying to yourself is necessary to preserve your self-esteem and your sanity. The act of repressing traumatic memories is a form of self-deception that your mind engages in for the purposes of self-preservation.

Generally, deception is a way of preserving your dignity and your safety. It also can serve as a social lubricant that preserves your reputation and your social relations with other people. If you lie to protect your pride, your reputation, your relationship, or anything else, you are lying for a legitimate reason. It may not be morally ideal, but it is still necessary. However, lying for other reasons crosses into darker territory. It is not really OK to lie to get what you want, but if you really need something, lying may be required. Certain jobs also call on the ability to be deceptive, such as politics or sales.

There are plenty of situations when deception is not necessary. Pathological lying and lying for no reason are forms of deception that are best avoided at all costs. When you lie too much, you damage your reputation. You also make it hard to keep track of your stories and avoid getting caught. You should never lie when you do not have to. Reserve deception for situations when honesty simply is not the best policy.

Deception is an engrained part of human nature. All people are born with the ability to lie. The ability starts to manifest quite early.

Scientists have found that deception starts in infancy, when babies fake hunger cries just so that their mothers will give them attention. From an early age, human beings start to realize that if they perform a certain action, they will receive a reward. As a result, they learn to fake actions and reactions that will get them what they want. This is the foundation of deception.

People never lose this ability to lie. Instead, they get better at it as they grow up. While some people are more deceptive than others, all people tend to want to lie to make themselves look better. They tell little white lies in social situations to be polite. They lie in poker or card games in order to win. They even lie to loved ones to avoid losing love. In fact, family members and romantic partners are often the worst liars to their loved ones because they want to look good to their loved ones and they also have the advantage of their loved ones' trust. Employees are also often prone to lying, as they attempt to win the boss's favor and perform well at work.

Sadly, many people find deception difficult, even though it is such an engrained part of human nature. Some people feel intensely guilty about lying. Others feel nervous and terrified of getting caught. Yet others are not able to come up with creative stories to fill in gaps in the truth. Whatever the reason, if you have trouble lying, you could greatly benefit by learning how to lie better. It is a good thing that you have picked up this book. You can develop the best deception skills to make anyone believe everything that you say.

You can enjoy many benefits from knowing the true art of deception. For instance, you can smooth out social situations with appropriate white lies. You can also sell things more easily and make yourself seem like a better person. Reality is yours to shape as you see fit. You will yield tremendous power after finishing this book.

Chapter 2: How You Give Yourself Away

Before I go into how to lie, I first want to discuss why you get caught lying. Understanding what makes you get caught lying can help you become a better liar. It can help you identify and cull out some of the tics that give away your dishonesty so that you no longer get caught.

When liars get caught, it is either because they got their stories confused, or because they gave away something called a tell. I will cover both in this chapter.

Tells

Lying is a stressful and emotionally strenuous activity. As a result, you act out in ways that are unusual when you engage in deception. Your guilt and nervousness may manifest in little tics known as tells. You may also struggle to think of a story, and as you do so, you give away little tells. Tells are just unusual little behaviors that indicate that you are being deceptive. Everyone has his or her own unique tell. You need to find yours, before your loved ones do. Chances are, your loved ones already know your tells and can spot exactly when you are lying as a result.

It is possible to stop giving yourself away by identifying and preventing your tell from manifesting when you lie. You need to become mindful of things you do when you lie. This can be hard, especially when in the heat of the moment. It may be a good idea to look into your memories and try to identify unusual things you do when you engage in deception. Think hard about how you feel when you lie and how it manifests in your body.

Common tells are usually physical twitches of some sort. Many people will start organizing the space around them. This is because the act of lying is messy, and so people freak out, trying to make everything neat and tidy. People may straighten papers on the table, or smooth out their clothes.

Self-grooming is another major tell. People may start inspecting and cleaning their nails, or messing with their hair. Watch for your hands; you may be surprised that they fly to your hair the minute you start to lie.

Nervous tics are another common tell. When someone is nervous, it will manifest in subtle physical cues. Stammering, biting nails, chewing on the insides of the lips, puckering the lips, picking at the face, picking at the insides of nails, and shaking one's foot are common nervous tics that betray deception. Twirling hair around the finger is another nervous tic that is common to people with longer hair. Try to relax and not betray yourself with lots of little nervous behaviors and tics like these.

Pauses are another huge tell. When you lie, you have to manufacture the story that you tell. This takes some effort and some thought. People who pause before answering a question are probably trying to come up with a convincing tale. Otherwise, they would just come out with the truth. Try to already have your lie planned out in advance, if possible, so that you do not have to pause. Also work on being more quick-witted and coming up with lies more rapidly so you don't give yourself away.

Eye Contact

The eyes communicate a lot nonverbally. Therefore, eye contact is a major giveaway in deception. People who are lying feel guilty or nervous and terrified of giving themselves away. They intuitively know that their eyes can give away their deception, so they have difficulty maintaining normal eye contact. Deceptive people will have either too much or too little eye contact.

It is best to believe your own lie. Then, you will have no problem with normal eye contact. If you cannot do this, at least try to just remember how eye contact normally is. You never stare directly into someone's eyes, nor do you hastily look away. You look at the general vicinity of their eyes as you speak.

Make sure that you do not rapidly drop your eyes. This is a normal reaction when you are lying because you are hastily scrambling to come up with something. But it is also a dead giveaway that you have something to hide. Resist this urge to look away and instead meet someone with normal eye contact at all times. This requires boldness, but that boldness will ultimately make you a more proficient liar.

Body Language

Your body language speaks more loudly than your words. You want to be very careful that you do not give away your dishonesty through your body language. Stiff, unnatural body language can give you away so try to stay relaxed. Also avoid doing anything unusual, like standing in an unusual posture. Specifically, you want to avoid grooming yourself, rubbing your hands together, fidgeting, or licking your lips. You want to also avoid turning a shoulder to the person you are lying to or avoiding eye contact with them. If you are sweaty out of nervousness, do not give it away by wiping frantically at your sweat. Keep your shoulders relaxed, uncross your legs and arms, keep your hands on the table in front of you or at your sides, and maintain normal eye contact. Relaxation and confidence are key when you are practicing deception, so do not let your shoulder tense up or your forehead crease with worry lines. Just act natural, like it is any other day.

Visual accessing cues

The direction that you look when you tell a lie can give you a way. When you look up to the right you are fabricating an image. When you look up to the left, you are recalling a picture that is already in your head. Therefore, if you are telling a lie, you will naturally want to look upward and right because you are imagining an image that does not already exist in your head. Avoid looking guilty by looking the opposite way or just maintaining normal-looking eye contact.

Hands

Recently, researchers have begun to question the idea that visual accessing cues give away when a person is lying. After surveying the eye movements of liars, some researchers say that visual accessing cues are inaccurate. However, the hands apparently never lie. One way you can spot a liar (or be spotted as a liar) is by moving and fidgeting your hands far too much. You are nervous, so you want to move. You want to groom yourself or organize the space around you. You may also want to make smoothing motions with your hands as you mentally smooth out details in your lie.

Changes in Tense

When people tell stories, they usually speak in the past tense. This is because the story occurred in the past and so it makes logical sense for the brain to assign a past tense to it. Usually, a story is comprised of three parts: a background, the main event, and the aftermath. If someone suddenly switches tenses at any one of these story elements, it is a good indicator that he or she is making something up. Something did not happen in the sequential order of the story, leading to the disruption in tense.

Often, liars will switch from the past tense to the present when they are lying. This is because the lie is presently forming in their mind, while the rest of the story really did occur as they say in the past. But any form of tense change is a giveaway.

Watch out for your tenses when you tell lies. Make sure you stay consistent throughout.

You want to stick to a certain tense to avoid arousing any kind of suspicion.

Passive Speaking

Passive speaking is one of the number one tells of deception. People who are running deception do not want to be direct. Directness is a sign of honesty and seems wrong to a liar, who is already guilty and nervous. It is physically difficult for a liar to stay direct in conversation. As a result, liars will choose to use passive, indirect language as a form of subterfuge.

Liars are more likely to use passive language that does not directly implicate themselves. For instance, someone who is lying might say, "The door got locked" instead of "I locked the door." In this way, the liar removes him- or herself from the statement.

Liars are also more likely to pick more passive words that lower the seriousness of an offense. For instance, a liar will be more likely to use the word "taken" rather than "stolen," and "killed" rather than "murdered."

Using more direct statements and terms can make you look like you are actually innocent. If you have the nerve to be direct and bold, then you probably are not lying. Or so other people will think. Remove the habit of passiveness from your lies and be more direct.

Answering a Question with a Question

As I have already showed you above, liars hate to be direct. Therefore, liars prefer not to answer questions definitively. It is easier for someone to answer a question with a question when being dishonest.

Think of this example. You are accused of stealing your roommate's favorite hair ribbon. When she confronts you, you say, "Do you really think I would steal something of yours?" You don't directly deny stealing it. Instead, you try to deflect guilt by answering her accusation with a question.

You will be far more convincing if you tell lies directly. Answer questions and accusations with direct statements, not questions. Do not act like you are hurt or indignant that you are being accused of something, either. Just deny whatever you are being accused of.

Too Many/Too Few Details

Details make up most of a story. They are what make a story seem believable or not. Keeping track of details is an important task when you are using deception. But watching details is also important.

Too few details makes you look like you are evading the truth. Too many details are also suspicious. You want to use a normal level of detail when you are lying. Think about how you normally tell stories. If you are lying to your spouse about taking a trip to the grocery store when really you went somewhere else, ask yourself how much you would usually divulge about a mundane trip to the grocery store. You probably wouldn't share many details, so don't share too many when you are lying. Yet if you are lying about work and you usually tell a lot of details about what you do during a work day, then you will want to share more details. Just remember the cardinal rule that I will discuss later: always be consistent.

You do not want to add too many miniscule details to a story. If you do, you may have trouble remembering these details later on. Keep only significant and relevant details in your stories.

Changing the Subject

When someone is lying, the sensation is usually uncomfortable. Therefore, liars want to get as far away from the conversation as possible. They are in a hurry to change the subject or even leave the room and stop talking. If you want to seem innocent, brazenly stick the conversation out. Lie as long as you have to, just so long as it does not look like you are fleeing the conversation. Do not abruptly change the subject.

If you do change the subject, make it a normal subject change onto a similar topic of conversation. For instance, if you are talking about what you did last night, don't change the subject to football. Instead, you can subtly change it to talk about some friend that you saw last night and something that is going on with him or her. This is a reasonable subject change because it is more or less on the same topic. It will not arouse suspicion but it will switch the lanes of the conversation.

Chapter 3: The Art of Deception

The art of deception is not as elusive or vague as you may imagine. In fact, it is relatively easy once you accept two fundamental truths. Understanding these truths can give you the ease of mind necessary so that you can relax and be convincing in your deception.

The first truth is that people are more open to truth than to skepticism. Especially loved ones actually *want* to believe you. When you tell someone something, you are following the conversational maxim that what you say is expected to be truthful. People are more likely to accept things you say as true without doubt, unless you have lied before or have a reputation as a dishonest person. Even then, you are still more likely to be believed than disbelieved. Doesn't that take a huge load off of your shoulders? Now you can relax when you lie, because most people are not normally searching for signs that you are lying. You have the advantage of trust on your side, especially with loved ones.

The second fundamental truth of deception is that you are innocent until proven guilty. You are the only one who knows for certain if you are lying or not. You have the power to disclose that fact, or lock it away where no one can ever find out. If you take control of this moment, you can ensure that no one is ever able to prove that you are guilty of lying. Even if someone suspects you of dishonesty or levels an accusation of dishonesty at you, they usually cannot prove it. You are in the clear until someone has solid proof of your deception. This solid proof is often hard to come by. You have the power to make sure that no one ever finds proof and you have the ability to make sure that you never get caught.

These two fundamental truths should make it relatively relieving. You have a great chance of getting away with any lie. You do not have to be so nervous, especially since nerves are usually what give you away. Now, read on for some excellent tips on how to lie believably and effectively. These tips will help you seize the power you have to not be caught.

Cardinal Rules

There are a few cardinal rules that you must memorize and follow in order to be successful at deception.

The first is that you must always be consistent. Behavior that is inconsistent with your normal behavior is best to be avoided. You want to act naturally, like you always do. This avoids arousing suspicion, especially in those who know you well. When it comes to lying to people who do not know you well, such as the police, you want to appear like you are behaving in a manner consistent with normal human behavior. People, particularly police, are often adept at spotting oddities in behavior. Strangers may actually be more able to spot when you are lying simply because the element of trust is not present as it is with people who know you well.

Therefore, you must be consistent at all times, no matter who you are lying to.

The second is that you should avoid lying when you don't really have to. Deception is a weapon that should be reserved for special situations. If you abuse deception, you end up losing your credibility. You also lose the trust of those around you. Choose your lies very carefully. Is something really worth lying over?

It is best to lie to loved ones only when you have a clear and unique need to. Usually, you only lie to loved ones to escape the restrictions that they place on you so that you can meet your own needs. If an opportunity presents itself that you cannot pass up, then you are driven to lie. But think very hard. Is this opportunity worth the risk of getting caught?

How much trouble would you be in if you just told the truth? Is the opportunity even worth taking?

Another cardinal rule is that lying involves risk. You are putting your relationship with someone on the line. You are also potentially risking your own reputation. Your lie better be good. Don't let this pressure make you nervous so that you flub up lies, however. Instead, use it as motivation to be very careful and very thorough in your deception so that you are never discovered.

It is important to keep in mind that you must never underestimate anyone. Never assume that someone is too dumb or too much of a stranger to catch you. Sometimes, the people who act the dumbest are in fact the most observant and the most intelligent. Watch out for the quiet ones – they are not talking because they are observing. Finally, strangers are the most emotionally detached from you and the most likely to raise questions and doubts about the veracity of what you say. Therefore, you are at risk of getting caught by anyone whom you deceive. Don't get cocky and let your guard down at any point. You have to tread quite carefully.

However, keep another rule in mind: While there is risk involved, you ultimately hold the power in all situations. The final cardinal rule of deception is this fact. If you are telling a lie, then you are holding onto a part of the truth. You are creating a false reality for someone else. You are even doing a little bit of dark manipulation on someone's mind. Basically, you are playing

God and creating your own piece of the world when you deceive someone. Keep this in mind. You are in a position of power, so use your power well. Do not let anyone take it from you. By holding onto your own power, you refuse to let others harm your ability to lie. You also have more confidence, which is always helpful in being effectively deceptive.

Never let these rules slip out of your mind when you decide to deceive someone. These rules can help establish your success as a liar and deceiver. These rules help you maintain your power, as well. Never let your power slip and you will be successful.

Tips and Tricks

Believe Your Own Lie

Sometimes it is crucial to believe your own lie. If you start by lying to yourself, you are less likely to give yourself away. This little trick is understood intuitively by pathological liars, who are able to create alternate realities in their minds where their lies are actually truths. Pathological liars have been found to more or less believe their own lies. Basically, this is a form of delusion. It is all part of the psychological phenomena which is pathological lying.

If you are not a pathological liar, it may seem impossible for you to do this. How can you believe something when you know in your heart that it is not true? It is possible to believe your own lies if you envision these lies in your mind like they are real memories. You can even try writing your lies down as if they were real. By visualizing your own lies, you help your mind absorb them. You basically commit them to memory. This makes the mind accept them and at least partially believe them. You can then make the conscious choice to relive your false memory, rather than your real one, when you tell a lie.

What if you confuse the truthful memory and the deceptive one? Well, focusing more on the deceptive memory will help prevent you from confusing the two. The lie will remain forefront in your mind if you think of it the most.

Practice It

Practicing your lie, or rehearsing it in your mind, is always a good idea. It helps you fill in the blanks so that you can tell the lie to someone convincingly, without pausing to think up details. It also helps you become more confident in the lie as you commit it to memory. Being confident makes you seem more honest and trustworthy to the person that you are deceiving.

Deception is really just acting. You are an actor, memorizing lines. You want to get your behavior and actions, or "blocking," down as well as the words. Just like an actor, you need to rehearse to get everything perfect. Do not be afraid to treat your lies as scenes or monologues and rehearse them. It will help you become a far more convincing and thorough liar.

Don't Give Away Tells

I already covered tells and giveaways in the previous chapter. I probably don't need to repeat it, but I will: Don't give away the fact that you are lying! Find and isolate your tells. Commit to acting naturally. Practicing and believing your own lies can definitely help you with that.

You should certainly try being more mindful of your behavior. Practice lying to yourself. Envision how you act while you lie to someone. Or go over your memories of lies that you have told, especially unsuccessful lies. Really hone in on how you look and act when you lie. These are the behaviors that need to go! Focus on recognizing when you engage in these behaviors and faithfully avoid them.

Focusing on these more deceptive behaviors is also a good idea. When you are busy using the behaviors outlined in the following tips, you will be less likely to engage in more telling behaviors.

Breathing Exercises for Relaxation

Breathing exercises can help you relax so that you are not a nervous wreck before you lie. There are certain exercises that you can perform that are very discreet. No one will suspect you of doing these exercises. They are often used by vocalists or performers before they get on stage, to help lessen stage fright.

One exercise is called belly breathing. Place a hand over your chest and a hand over your upper stomach. Now draw breath deep,

deep into your belly. Feel your stomach walls expand outwards. Your upper stomach should be pressing against your hand. Exhale quickly through your mouth. Now repeat four times, or as many times as necessary to get all of your anxiety and nervousness out.

You can also breathe through your nose and out through your mouth. Focus on the sensation of the breath coming in through your nasal passages and then going out of your throat. Count your breaths for a few cycles. This should definitely calm your nerves and relax you.

Another calming breath is to breathe in and hold it as you count one thousand and one, one thousand and two, one thousand and three, on thousand and four. On the last count, release your breath. This makes your entire body begin to release tension through breath. It also fills your muscles with oxygen so that you feel calmer and more invigorated.

Confidence

Confidence is key to getting away with deception. If you appear confident, people will not suspect you of lying. They will be more likely to accept you as an authority who speaks truth. You want to project confidence and authority in every way possible.

The best way to project confidence is through your posture. Stand tall, with your spine straight. Hold your head up straight. Do not slouch or cower. When you adopt a more confident posture, you will naturally become more confident. You will seem like someone who has nothing to hide. People will be more inclined to believe the words that you utter if you seem confident and sure of what you are saying.

Be Discerning

Again, take a great trick from pathological liars: Develop a sense about people. Some people will believe certain lies, while others will not. Being savvy about who to lie to is a good idea. You will avoid getting caught that way.

In addition, you can easily tell what types of lies will work on certain people if you hone your character discernment skills. For instance, insecure people will fall for lies that somehow bolster their suffering egos. Learn to scan people quickly to find out what lies will appeal to them.

Be Consistent

This is one of the cardinal rules. It is so important that I want to go over it again. You may have some questions about how to be consistent. There are many areas in your communication where you may be inconsistent without meaning to be.

If you act inconsistent in your behavior, you give away your dishonesty. If your words do not match the emotions in your face and body language, then you raise others' suspicions. You also must maintain consistency in the details of your stories so that you do not give away the fact that you are lying. A changing story is always one of the surest giveaways that you are not being fully truthful.

When you lie, you must try to act like you always do to avoid setting off alarm bells for people who know you well. You must maintain consistency in behavior while you lie as well. Make sure that you look sad if your story is sad. Keep your posture and body language relaxed and natural. Make sure that your stories remain consistent. Consistency is easy when you believe your lie and when you believe that you are doing nothing wrong. Keeping the details of your story at a minimum is also helpful so that you can remember your lie and keep it the same.

Plan Your Lie

Lies that are well-planned usually are more convincing, psychologists say. Lies require you to jump over some ethical hurdles and think of a convincing story. This is difficult and stressful.

First, create excellent alibis if you can. Set up a routine so that you can explain where you were at a certain time. Get people to lie for you, if you can. Take the time you need to fabricate a wonderfully convincing lie with a solid background that will check out.

Second, invest time in fabricating a beautiful and convincing story. Then commit to that story, no matter what. You can always think of ways to defend your story or fill in the blanks if you commit to it. Be sure that your story is logical and believable, and also make sure that you do not create too many details. Too many details make it hard to keep track of your story.

Third, prepare for the worst. What will you do if you get caught? Have this firmly rehearsed. Have multiple fallback options.

Having fallback options will help you feel more confident so that you will be less nervous and scared when you tell a lie.

Follow Conversational Rules

When using deception, you want to appear as normal as possible. One way to do this is to have normal conversation. There are certain rules, known as conversational maxims, which will help you with this.

The first rule is the maxim of quality. This is where people expect you to be honest. You can take advantage of this by expecting people to believe you. This expectation works because it makes you appear more confident. You can also rest assured that most people will buy what you say in conversation if you do not provide any cause for doubt.

The second is the maxim of quantity. People expect you to reveal a normal level of detail, not too little or too much. You want to avoid seeming vague by providing some detail, but you also want to appear normal by not going manic with details.

The third rule is the maxim of relation, which means that you stay on topics that are related to your original conversation topic. Abruptly changing the subject is suspicious and abnormal. If you want to change the subject, change it to something related to what you were already talking about.

The final rule involves the maxim of manner, which means that your answers should be direct and to the point. Vague or weird answers can be really suspicious because people don't follow you. You want to say things that people can easily follow. If you don't, you look like a liar.

Always follow these maxims when you speak with others to avoid arousing suspicion. Your conversation will seem normal, and people will not suspect you of lying as a result. You never want to talk too little or too much, use unclear phrases, change the subject abruptly, or provide obviously erroneous answers. If you violate any of these conversational rules, you can arouse a lot of suspicion about your integrity and the motives lying underneath your conversation.

You can flip these conversational maxims around and use them to mislead people. You can use the maxim of relations and change the subject rapidly, giving others the hint that you do not want to follow the line of conversation anymore. This subject change can imply to people that you are not willing to discuss the matter anymore. You can also use the maxim of manner to say something purposefully vague. For instance, if someone asks you "How you do I look in this dress?" you don't have to lie and say that she looks great. You can instead say, "You look interesting."

You can also use the maxim of quantity to tell a lie by omission. You give just enough information that it makes your conversation partner feel like you are telling the truth. But you leave out something. While this is technically lying, you can also claim, "I forgot" or "I didn't think it was important" if your omission is ever found out.

Obscure Details

When using deception, it is best to be a little bit vague. The fewer details you mention, the fewer things you need to keep track of in order to keep your stories straight. You then run less of a risk of giving yourself away by messing up a tiny detail later on. People often forget small details, but you will be surprised what people can remember, especially if they suspect you of lying. You never want to give someone any little thing that they can remember and use against you later on. Therefore, being vague protects you from giving yourself away.

You also have fewer details to think of while making up a lie. This can make lying easier. Just focus on creating the bare bones details and then moving on. You can blame incorrect or left-out details on your faulty memory.

Use Affection and Physical Closeness

When you are lying to loved ones, maintaining affection and physical closeness are great ways to give the appearance of honesty. You can seem trustworthy if you are affectionate. Offer reassuring touch and hugs to your loved ones as you lie, and do everything you can to ingratiate yourself with them. By touching your loved ones, you give the sensation that you have nothing to hide and you are being upfront.

You do not want to do this in a way that is inconsistent with your normal behavior. As I said before, consistency is crucial to avoid arousing suspicion. If you are not normally a physically affectionate person or you have a loved one who does not like to be touched much, then disregard this advice.

Physically touching can also help you lie to the opposite sex. You can turn the touching into flirting. Just a brief arm touch or hand grab is enough to give someone the idea that you are interested. This can distract him or her from what you are really saying, and it will make him or her want to like you and help you.

Don't Wait to Be Asked

Volunteer information right away without waiting to be asked. This will make you seem like you are being upfront. It also gives you the momentum to create and perpetuate a lie. Hesitation is not favorable when lying. It makes you look less believable.

Let's say you want to lie about what you did the night before. When you walk into your house in the morning, just immediately launch into a story about your night. Don't slink off to the bedroom or bathroom to hide and do not avoid conversation.

Be Direct

The more direct you are, the better your lie will be. I already talked about avoiding passiveness when you lie. Take this a step further and actually use very direct language. Call attention to yourself. Be open. You will be the last person that everyone suspects if you act like this.

Take this extreme example. You accidentally destroy someone's favorite piece of furniture, a chair. When the person comes home, immediately start a speech about how disrespectful people are and how you can't believe someone smashed that chair.

Lie to Yourself

You probably already lie to yourself to a degree. Humans are masters at self-deception. When confronted with a truth that you are not comfortable with, you may distort this truth totally. You may repress memories and emotions. This self-deception protects your mind from harm. While it is not always effective at healing your mental wounds, it can be very useful in the art of deception. I will cover this more in a later chapter, but I recommend using self-deception as a means to get better at lying.

Psychologists say that people who engage in self-deception are overall better liars. Pathological liars are the best at quickly and shamelessly convincing themselves that their lies are true. You can use this to make yourself better at lying by practicing on yourself. You should also lie to yourself so that you can believe your lie wholeheartedly.

You can convince yourself of the truth of a lie that you are telling. When you at least partially believe the lie, you are more likely to indicate that with your body language and speech. Therefore, you become more convincing and you calm down your nervous tells.

Build in a Good Reputation

If you are known as someone who is unfailingly honest, then people are less likely to think that you are lying. You want to try to create a clean track record as an honest and good person.

This is part of why it is very important to not lie too much. If you lie too much, you get the reputation as a liar. This reputation is very difficult to shake. Instead, build your reputation as an honest person. People will look to you as an authority and will trust you more openly.

Mix in Some Truth

The very best lies are hard to catch because they contain bits of truth. Truthful details can serve you well because they can mislead people from suspecting or disbelieving the dishonesty that you have also uttered. People might verify one or two things as true, and so they believe you.

Make sure that your lie is at least fifty percent truth. Add in as many truthful details as possible. This will make your lie seem honest. The more details you include that can be reasonably verified, the more likely you will get away with your deception. You will also feel better about your lie, so you will be less likely to give away any tells.

You can also lie by omission. Tell the truth, but omit a few details. If someone confronts you about lying, just claim, "I didn't lie. I just forgot to mention that." It is even better to use manipulation and claim, "I didn't lie. You just didn't ask." Make it seem like someone else's fault if you are caught lying by omission. Really, lying by omission is deception, but you can easily make it look like it is not your fault.

Put Pressure on Someone

You can put pressure on people to convince them that they have to believe you. By putting pressure on somebody, you can take away their ability to discern if you are lying or telling the truth. Hurry someone along or act irritable when they question you. Do not give them time to ask questions or pay attention to too many details.

There are many ways to put pressure on someone. You can use guilt and remind people of all the nice things you have done for them in the past. "Why would you think I am lying to you? After all I have done for you?"

You can use the excuse that you have no time for this. Or pretend that you are in a major hurry. Hurry someone along with you to hide your deception.

Tell People what They Want to Hear

People are selective listeners. This means that they choose to hear what they want to hear. You can tell people lies and let them pick out the details that they are bound to like. Details that boost their egos are sure to work. Figure out what someone wants to hear and then casually leave out other details or lead them to make their own conclusions. Then, it is their own fault if they reach the wrong conclusions based on what you say. You are in the clear for lying.

Take this example. A friend asks you if a guy you both know likes her. You know he doesn't like her but you do not want to hurt her feelings, so you vaguely mention that he seemed to be looking at her. She will hear, "He likes you" from this.

Chapter 4: Lying to Yourself

Lying to yourself is usually a bad idea. But at times, it can help you avoid emotional harm and pain. It can also help you handle situations that are too hard for you to deal with. In some cases, self-deception acts as a life saver. In other situations, it is harmful. This chapter will help you learn how to deal with self-deception.

Why Lie to Yourself?

Self-deception can be harmful when you are repressing emotions and memories that you actually should be experiencing. Lying to yourself all of the time borders on being delusional. But self-deception has also been found to be crucial to your mental health and your success in areas of life such as business.

One form of self-deception that is especially helpful is called positivity bias. Children as young as three years old have a tendency toward positivity bias. This is when you see yourself in a more positive way and you ignore your more negative aspects. You think that your work and your accomplishments are great and you fail to see the flaws in what you do. When you do something bad, you tend to lessen its severity compared to other people. For instance, if you shoplift something, you tend to be able explain it away as not that big of a deal, but if someone else steals the same item from the same store, you would judge him or her harshly for stealing. This concentration on your positive attributes helps boost your self-esteem. A preoccupation with your negative traits is the hallmark of depression and low self-esteem, so you can actually benefit from having positivity bias.

Lying to yourself about how you look to other people can also help you succeed. If you tell yourself that you do not care about what others think, you become immune to the insecurities that can easily plague your relationships. People often feel the need to lie to themselves about their attributes in order to feel fit for dating relationships. It is better to lie to yourself to get rid of certain insecurities that lower your confidence and hence your quality of life.

It is often a good idea to lie to yourself when it comes to succeeding at something. You should believe in yourself and your abilities.

When you convince your mind that you are capable of completing a certain task, then you are more likely to be able to, against all odds. For instance, believing that you are a great public speaker can help you deliver a speech at least adequately.

When something crumbles your self-esteem, sometimes self-deception can help you rebuild your ego. You can lie to yourself that what happened is not your fault. You can say things like, "His/her loss" or "He/she will regret choosing someone else over me." You release the pain by denying your fault in the situation. In certain ego-shattering events, this is the only way that you can preserve your self-love and begin the healing process.

How to Lie to Yourself

How do you lie to yourself? It is easier than you imagine. Self-deception works because your mind is incredibly sensitive to manipulation. If you tell yourself something long enough, your mind will start to believe it, at least at some surface level. You may know the truth deep in your subconscious mind, but you do not have to think about the truth at all.

When you want to believe something badly enough, it is a good idea to envision it hard in your mind. Envision it being reality. Envision living in this alternate, desirable state. The more time you spend fantasizing about this ideal state, the more real it will seem to your mind. You will come to accept it as true.

You can also refuse to think about the truth. This is known as repression. When the truth begins to bubble up in your mind, hastily dismiss it. Think of your self-lie instead. This will bury the truth in a place where you do not have to think about it too much.

The best way to alter reality for yourself is to act and speak like your lie is true. This will convince your mind and this will convince others around you to reflect your lie as truth. It will become real for everyone. You can even write about your self-deception in your journal to make it more real to yourself.

How to Stop Lying to Yourself

Before I discussed the many reasons that self-deception is beneficial. But there are plenty of cases where it does not serve you well at all. Ending self-deception can be hard, especially when it has become a habit for you. Self-deception is often very comforting so ending it can jerk you out of your comfort zone unpleasantly.

One of the main times that self-deception stops serving you any benefit at all is when you keep lying to yourself about a relationship. You tell yourself that you are happy or that you are safe. You deny the abuse or hurt that is being done to you, or you deny how the relationship is just not working out and you are fighting too hard to make it work. You may be engaging in self-deception about a job or other life situation in the same manner, as well.

You may also be deceiving yourself about who you are. You fail to notice or acknowledge flaws so you have no way to improve yourself.

You limit yourself and exist in a state of denial. Often, it is necessary to be brutally honest with yourself for any type of self-growth and exploration to take place.

When you keep lying to yourself like this, you are preventing yourself from finding out the truth. If the truth is uncomfortable, that is just a sign that you need to work on something in your life or yourself. Not doing so keeps you trapped in a bad place in life. You never grow. Sometimes, self-deception provides you with a cocoon of comfort and safety that is non-conducive to your overall happiness as a human being. Break out of the habit when it stops serving you well. Embrace the truth, no matter how much it hurts, and use the pain to start making some necessary changes to your existence.

You also begin to damage your interpersonal relationships when you are not honest with yourself. Your self-deception will manifest in many ways that can be hurtful to your loved ones. You also can be very unhappy because your life does not meet your secret expectations. This unhappiness will be apparent to the people who know you well, and they will suffer watching you suffer.

The first step to stopping self-deception is to notice when you are engaging in it. A good sign that you are not being honest with yourself is when you notice a mismatch in your emotions. This is when you *should* be happy about something...but you are not. This is when you *should* trust your romantic partner because he treats you wonderfully and has never made you doubt his loyalty, yet you are full of misgivings and trust issues. This is when you say you love your job, yet you can barely get out of bed in the mornings because you just dread another day at the office. If your emotions sharply mismatch what you tell yourself, there is something wrong. Your emotions are harming you but you are refusing to acknowledge them and fix whatever is causing the pain for you.

Also, notice your automatic thoughts. What first pops into your head when something happens? This automatic thought is your initial gut reaction. It is usually accurate to what you really think and feel. If you are lying to yourself, you probably have lots of thoughts where you think, "No, why would I think that?" These thoughts are not aligned with your self-deception and thus cause you great confusion. You must work to repress mismatched thoughts.

Notice your behavior. You may claim that you are not a jealous person, yet you check your significant other's phone now and then to see if he is cheating. You do not want to think that you hate someone, yet you find yourself acting in petty ways and puffin yourself up to be intimidating whenever that person comes around. These little strange moments of mismatched behavior indicate your true thoughts and feelings. If you act in strange ways, you may want to really analyze your thoughts and feelings and admit some hard truths to yourself.

It is also a good idea to start being honest with yourself in the future. When you start to reassure yourself of some lie, recognize that you are just lying to yourself. Your genuine, automatic emotions are probably the honest truth. Listen to your gut emotions and automatic thoughts. Choose to be honest with yourself and to not lie.

Chapter 5: What to Do If You are Caught Lying

Ideally, you will never face the problem of getting caught. Especially if you follow the tips in this book, your chances of getting caught are quite minimal. However, it is best to always prepare for the worst scenario possible. Having a backup plan is a good way to help make yourself more confident, anyway, since you will know that you are prepared.

Lie More

It is always possible to lie more to make a previous lie seem true. If you are caught in a lie, explain your lie away with another lie. Or else say, "I'm sorry, I lied," and come up with another lie posed as the truth. Once you start a lie, it is usually best to commit to that lie fully and stick it out to the very end. Coming clean is not always the best idea, especially since you have already lied and you stand to get in trouble.

But the problem with this is that lying more and more only gets you into a deep hole. You will soon catch yourself in a web of confusing and even conflicting lies. It is possible that you will forget what you have told people, and you will get caught. Before you get in over your head, really ponder if lying more will solve your problems. You should only use more lying as a means to escape the truth if the truth is truly horrible.

Manipulate

It can be useful to manipulate someone in various ways to save face or prevent issues and consequences when you are caught lying. Manipulation is the action of using someone's emotions to elicit a desired reaction from him or her. It is incredibly effective and can get you out of any lie if you employ it correctly.

A great politician's trick is to deflect your guilt. If someone accuses you of lying, just bring up something that he or she did wrong to you in the past. Bring up that time your spouse lied to you years ago, for instance. You want to put someone on the defensive. People hate being attacked for what they do wrong, so if you point out someone's wrongdoing, you can make that person forget all about accusing you because he or she will be focused on defending him or herself.

It is often useful to keep a few things in your back pocket to whip out in dire situations, such as when you are caught lying. For instance, if your loved one lies to you, do not immediately confront him or her. Just keep your knowledge of the falsehood in the back of your mind. Then, if you ever get into trouble for lying yourself, bring it up. You will surprise your loved one so much with your unrevealed knowledge that you will deflect all attention away from yourself.

You can also manipulate your accuser's emotions by playing the victim. Act like it is your accuser's fault that you lied in the first place. Mention that you felt that you had to lie because your accuser never lets you be yourself or tend to your own needs. Indicate an array of hurt emotions – even cry if you have to. Distract attention away from what you did wrong by making it seem like you are actually the one in pain.

You can use gas lighting, a form of mental abuse, to make your accuser believe that he or she is insane. Firmly and steadfastly deny that you lied. Even if there is solid proof, continue denying it. Even deny that the proof someone is confronting with you is real. Eventually, you will become convincing. Say something enough times and people will start to believe it.

A final effective form of manipulation is to play off the severity of your lie. If you act like it is no big deal and refuse to acknowledge that someone else finds it to be a big deal, then you can manipulate someone into thinking that he or she is overreacting. You can even dismiss his or her emotions and say things like, "You are majorly overreacting. You shouldn't be so upset. People lie all the time, so get over it."

No, these methods are not nice. But lying is not nice, either. If you do not feel comfortable using manipulation when you get caught lying, then consider offering an apology.

Apologize

Are you ready to truly admit that you lied? Is there no chance of redemption? Is there no way to preserve your pride and your appearance of honesty? Are you just tired of lying and fighting? If you have reached the point where you answered yes to any of those questions, then perhaps it is time to simply apologize. Back down, drop your ego, and say that you are sorry.

You do not have to offer an explanation unless someone asks for one. Sometimes, not offering an explanation is the best course of action. Just apologizing is often enough to start the healing process and to put a lie behind you.

You have the right to ask for forgiveness, but you are not entitled to it. There is a chance that you will not be forgiven for lying. It is an unfortunate reality. This is why you need to carefully consider if deception is even worth it before you lie.

Learn when to Admit Defeat

Sometimes, giving up a lie and admitting defeat is necessary. There are times when you just cannot keep up a lie up. But when is it time? Often, you will just know. However, it is not always so simple. You need to learn when to admit defeat so that you can avoid using bad judgment and prolonging a lie past when you should.

It is a good idea to finally just admit defeat when your relationship with someone is at stake. Lying is really not worth jeopardizing love. If your lover knows the truth and you are hurting him or her by keeping the lie up, it is time to admit defeat.

It is also a good idea to admit defeat when you get in too deep. If you have to keep telling lie after lie just to keep one little lie afloat, then it is causing more stress than it is worth. Maybe it is just time to admit defeat. The consequences of lying are probably not going to be as terrible as you imagine in your mind.

Is something valuable at stake? Such as your job or your reputation? You may want to save face by gracefully admitting that you lied. You can offer an explanation for your dishonorable behavior if you feel that it will lessen the severity of the consequences. But sometimes, exhibiting the courage that it takes to come out with the truth is valuable in itself.

Chapter 6: How to Tell When Someone is Lying to You and What to Do What About It

It takes one to know one, they say. If you are successful liar, or if you have at least studied deception, then you are better prepared to spot liars. You now know the signs to watch for after reading how to lie. But what do you do when someone lies to you? With your trust shattered and your ego buffeted by a strong sense of betrayal, it can be hard to use good judgment and handle situations well when you catch someone deceiving you. But there are things that you can do to make the situation more straightforward.

How to Spot Liars

I will go over some telltale signs of lying with you. Use these signs to spot when someone is telling you a lie.

First of all, you have a strong gut instinct. You probably are already adept at telling when someone is being not-quite-honest. But you may deny it to yourself, especially if the person is a loved one. You prefer to believe that the person is being honest and you are just being paranoid. Well, here is good news and bad news: You are never just being paranoid. That gut feeling that you are being deceived is probably one hundred percent accurate. This is good news because it means that you can catch liars in your life, but it is bad news because you are probably not wrong when you get that weird feeling in your gut.

Say you can't tell if your weird gut feeling is true or not, however. You are riddled with doubt. In that case, there are some signs that you should watch for in people that give away their dishonesty.

Remember how I talked about tells? Watch people for tells when you are interrogating them. The major tells to watch for include self-grooming, fidgeting, nail biting, nail picking, clothes straightening, hair neatening, lip chewing, and other strange little habits. Also watch for hesitating, and weird eye contact. Watch for when people switch tenses or use really passive, vague language. Sweating is a huge sign that someone is feeling nervous. Why are they so nervous if they are being honest? Watch for excessive sweating and skin wiping.

You should also take notice when someone pauses while speaking. This pause indicates that he or she is searching for what to say next and is not being fully honest with you.

You should also be relentless in your pursuit of the truth. Your relentlessness will make liars incredibly nervous. Liars will be more likely to slip up with the truth or to confess if you seem like you are ruthless. Keep track of details and ask about variances in details or deviations from the original story. Drill someone with questions. Act tough.

Repeat questions again and again. Liars will probably slip up and change their story. Watch for changes in details. That is a dead giveaway that they are lying.

You can even claim that you know the real truth. This is called bluffing. It is a good way to make people nervous and make them spit out the truth. Some people may call your bluff; pretend to ignore it when they try to do this. It is probably just a ploy to break down your defenses and convince you that they are not lying.

Why Loved Ones Lie to You

Your loved ones make life worth living. But they can also cause you a lot of emotional pain. Your loved ones are way more likely to tell you lies than people that you barely know. Suspect your loved ones above anyone else for deception. They are the ones who will betray you, and they will make it hurt.

Loved ones are so likely to lie to you because they feel that they must. Loving relationships tend to put more constraints on people. Therefore, people do not want to upset their loved ones but they want to do as they please. So they do what they want to do and then lie about it. Think about it. Probably most of the lies that you have been told where by significant others or children who wanted to go out and do something that you disapproved of. You have control over your loved ones, so they lie in order to shirk the control without upsetting you or losing your love.

This form of lying is very selfish. But it is also very normal. Your loved ones want to have their cake and eat it too. The fact that you love one another also creates a relationship of trust that makes it very easy for deception to take place. Above all, you are more likely to forgive deception by loved ones, and your loved ones know this.

Read on to find out how to curb loved ones lying to you.

How to Confront Liars without Being Lied to More

What should you do when you catch someone in a lie? Well, the first and most obvious tip is to not get too tangled up in emotions. You undoubtedly will feel a great deal when you are lied to, but emotions can make you go off the wall. It is better to be calm, cool, and collected so that you can think straight.

First, try to empathize with the liar. Would you have lied in the same position? Why do you feel the person felt the need to lie to you? Taking this time to empathize can help remove some of the fury and hurt from the occasion. You understand why someone lied and that makes it easier to accept the lie. You can get over it more easily. You can also have a discussion with the person who lied to you about why he or she lied and how you can move past the lie together.

Second, ask if this lie is a big deal. If it is something small, you have the right to be upset about it. But understand that if you make a tiny white lie a huge deal, the person will actually be more inclined to lie to you more in the future to avoid your dramatic temper. You are not discouraging people from lying to you by taking drastic action over every little lie.

Third, open lines of communication. Being accusing only warrants a defensive reaction. Prevent defensiveness by saying something like, "I know that you lied to me. That really hurts me. But I want to talk about why you felt the need to lie to me. I don't hate you and I'm not mad, just hurt." When you approach this confrontation more gently, the liar will be more inclined to work with you and to not tell you more lies. You can actually make progress and even prevent future deception, which I will cover more in the proceeding section.

Confronting liars should be calm and devoid of emotions like anger. Seeing anger will often trigger a liar to lie to you more to avoid your temper. But you can diffuse the situation by being calm. It is a good idea to show how hurt you are. If the person who lied to you is not a psychopath, then he or she will probably feel guilty. Guilt is a far more effective way to get people to stop lying to you than fear or any other emotion. Try to evoke as much guilt as possible.

Do not let liars use deflection on you. A liar might tell you, "Yeah, well, you did this to me so –" Cut him or her off right there. Say quite frankly that you can talk about that later, but right now the topic of discussion is on the deception. Keep the conversation on point and do not allow the liar to shift focus off of him or herself.

It can be beneficial if you reach an agreement to prevent future lying. You may both have to compromise. Say your spouse keeps lying to you because she wants to go to a club that you don't approve of, since it is a club for singles. You don't approve, yet she keeps going because all of her friends go. She lied to you about going to the club. Now, you can make an agreement where you let her go to the club, as long as she promises to check in with you often and not flirt with single guys there. Think of compromises like this where you loosen the reigns so that your loved one stops feeling the need to lie to you. Use dishonesty as a sign that changes are in order in your relationship.

There comes a point in a relationship where you might want to consider cutting off further contact. Lying is a part of human nature and you will probably be lied to multiple times by loved ones. But excessive lying indicates that someone has no respect for your emotions or your dignity as a human being. Someone who continually tells you big, hurtful lies is probably not going to stop, especially if you have asked him or her to stop in the past to no avail. You do not have to tolerate this type of relationship. You should consider how valuable the relationship is to you and determine if it is worth the emotional pain that comes with it. Sometimes, even if it hurts, you need to end the relationship. You are preserving your own dignity while teaching a pathological liar a good lesson about the consequences of lying too much. You may just be doing the liar a favor as well as yourself.

How to Discourage People from being Dishonest with You

You can limit how much people lie to you by taking certain steps in how you treat people. The way you phrase questions and the consequences you offer for transgressions can all play a role in how honest your loved ones are with you. While it is not your fault when people lie to you, how you act can really influence whether or not people are honest around you.

If you are constantly being lied to, you may want to consider that you are being overly harsh and strict. Relaxing your rules on your loved ones may help them feel more comfortable telling you the honest truth. Relationships and love are not about control; relinquishing control is sometimes necessary for the health of a relationship. Consider how important your rules really are and drop some of the more unreasonable ones.

Your temper may be another driving factor in how much your loved ones lie to you. They may be so intimidated by your temper that they feel the need to lie to you all of the time. Try to be more understanding. Then, people will feel more comfortable talking to you and being honest with you. Become more of a conversationalist than a disciplinarian. When your loved ones see that you do not just explode over things, they will want to talk to you more and hide things from you less.

On the other hand, though, you should offer very strict consequences for pathological lying. If there is no good reason for a lie or someone keeps hurting you by lying to you, do not tolerate it. You should never just let lies slip. A great consequence for this is to just stop talking to the person who continually lies to you. Cut this disrespectful deception out of your life for good.

You can be scary by keeping certain lies to yourself. Only reveal that you know the truth at opportune moments. Do not express anger, just reveal that you have been aware of the truth for a while. This will give liars in your life heart attacks. It will also make them afraid to lie to you more, since you have such good radar. You may get people to be more honest with you this way.

Conclusion

You have now reached the end of your guide to the art of deception. You are now knowledgeable about the many ways to lie to others and to yourself. You have also developed a stellar lie detector that can smell lies from ten miles away and catch liars in the act. Deception is no longer an elusive secret, but rather an art that you are the master of.

Remember that deception is just like theatre. You are putting on a performance. The more stellar your performance, the more likely people will believe your lie. You can avoid a lot of trouble if you put on a believable and realistic performance. So break a leg.

You can have a lot of fun with deception. You can remove the fear that makes deception so nerve-wracking and difficult. You can also remove the guilt because there is a good reason that you need to lie. Instead of giving yourself away with little tells, you can lie boldly and comfortably. No one will ever suspect you of being less than truthful.

There are many tips and tricks that can help make you a better liar. Review this book whenever you find your deception skills are slipping. But the main trick is to just act like yourself. Put on a show that is consistent with your normal behavior. As a result, you will have a more convincing performance deceiving others.

You can practice deception on strangers. Try telling people that you have never met bizarre and outlandish stories about yourself and who you are. By lying this way, you can start to get used to the sensation of lying.

Thank you for reading!

Other great books by Madison Taylor on Kindle, paperback and audio

Rejection Proof Therapy 101: How To Overcome, Deal With And Heal Yourself From Rejection

Cognitive Behavioral Therapy For Beginners: How To Use CBT To Overcome Anxieties, Phobias, Addictions, Depression, Negative Thoughts, And Other Problematic Disorders

Forbidden Psychology 101: The Cool Stuff They Didn't Teach You About In School

Escaping the Introvert World: The Introvert's Guide To Overcoming Shyness, Social Anxiety, And Fear To Thrive In An Extrovert World

NLP For Beginners: Learn the Secrets of Self Mastery, Developing Magnetic Influence and Reaching Your Goals Using Neuro-Linguistic Programming

Depression Proof Yourself: How To Avoid And Overcome Being Depressed

Love Thyself: The First Commandment to Raising your Self Esteem, Boosting your Self-Confidence, and Increasing your Happiness

The Art of Decision Making: How to Make Better Choices in Love, Life, and Work

The Dark Science of Psychological Warfare: How To Always Keep The Upper Hand On Anyone Psychologically

Staying Focused: How to Effectively Eliminate the Weapons of Mass Distraction

Turbo Charged NLP: A New and Improved Way of Taking Self Mastery, Influence, and Neuro-linguistic Programming to the Next Level

Made in the USA
San Bernardino, CA
03 July 2017